For Max & Archie, with love – C.R.
For Ray & Pat – A.J.

A TEMPLAR BOOK

First published in the UK in hardback in 2001 by Templar Publishing
This edition published in 2002 by Templar Publishing,
an imprint of The Templar Company plc,
Pippbrook Mill, London Road, Dorking, Surrey, RH4 1JE, UK
www.templarco.co.uk

Distributed in the UK by Ragged Bears Ltd.,
Ragged Appleshaw, Andover, Hampshire, SP11 9HX

ISBN 1-84011-104-6

Edited by Marcus Sedgwick
Designed by Mike Jolley

Printed in Belgium by Proost

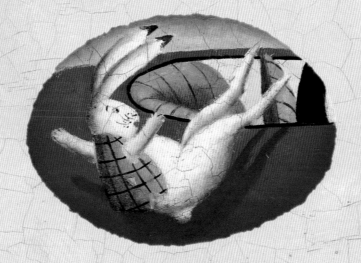

The Race

CAROLINE REPCHUK • Illustrated by ALISON JAY

templar publishing

HONK! Growled Hare, really wild, but Tortoise simply stopped and smiled.

"Whoa there, Bunny! In a hurry?
The speed you're going just isn't funny!
Slow and steady is the way to get somewhere without delay.

Think that's all just silly talk? Well I am heading for New York.
Perhaps," said Tortoise, "you would care,
to have some fun and race me there?"

"Fine," said Hare, "I like a race!"
A route was set, they made a bet, and so began a famous chase...

Now Tortoise was really taking his time,
as Hare revved up on the starting line.

"See you in New York, I trust?"

And away he **hared** in a cloud of dust.

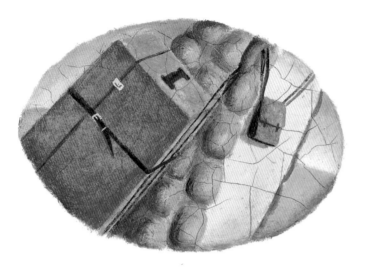

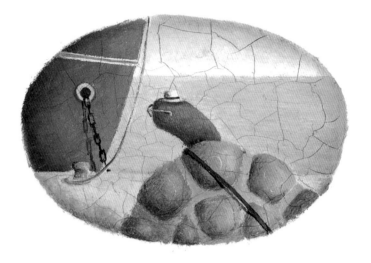

But Tortoise had a simple plan...

...and so he waved goodbye to land.

Now Hare had set off at the double,

but very soon
ran into trouble...

Travelled through Europe
with some delay.
I'm off to Africa today..
Trying new transport.
Will write soon,
As long as I learn
to land my balloon...

To
Pig and Goose
The White Cliffs,
England.

Hare was floating higher and higher,
Till his ears brushed the flames and caught on fire.
Poor old Hare! He started to frown, for what goes up
must come down...

And as he crawled across the sand, suitcase held tightly in his hand,
The only thing that he could **think**, was,

"GOSH! I really need
a drink, of...

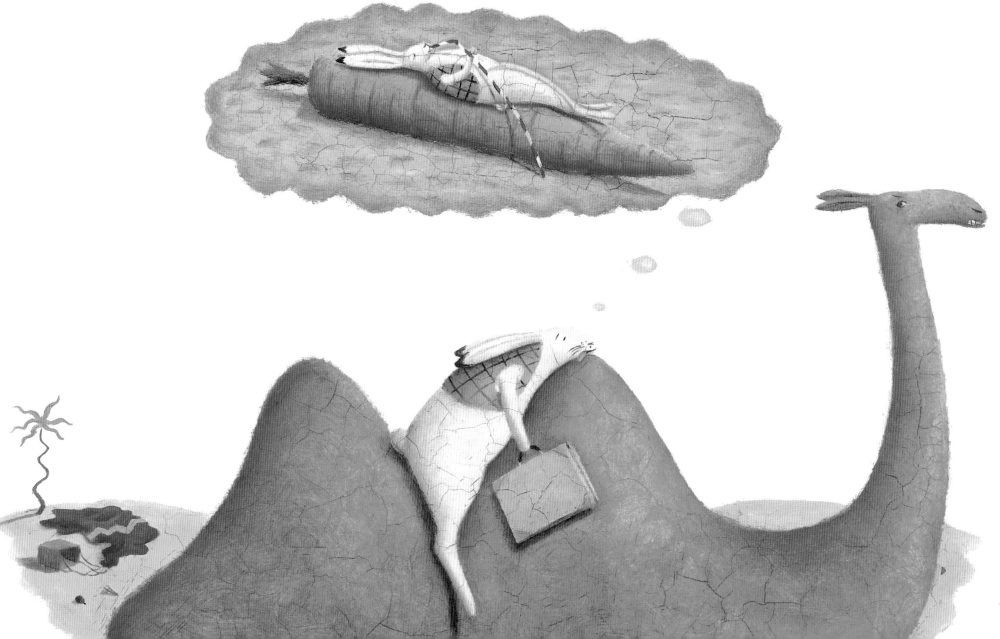

Soon a river and canoe
Stopped poor Hare from feeling blue.
Until, that is, he went
too far

(While Tortoise fished in Zanzibar)...

Hare **shot** down the raging river, past clutching **claws**,

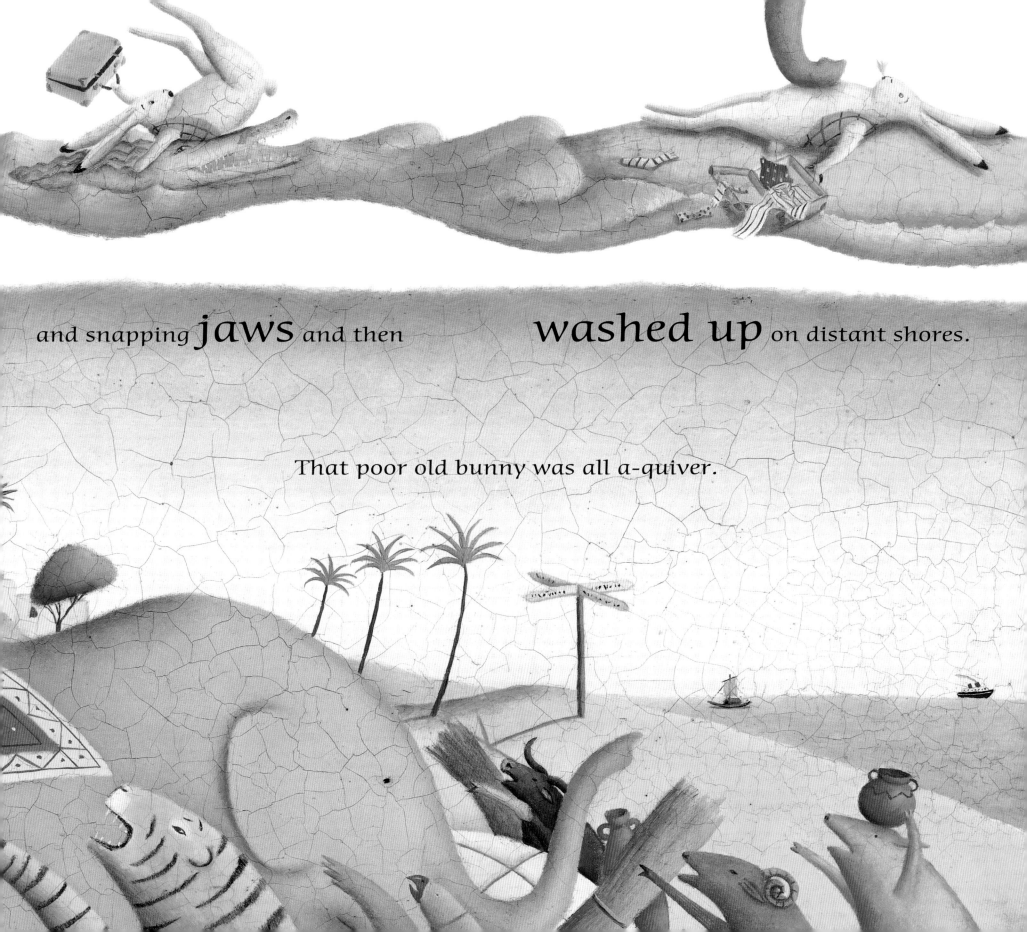

and snapping jaws and then washed up on distant shores.

That poor old bunny was all a-quiver.

Hare was doing really badly,
and next he found himself quite sadly
on a sampan
bound for China.

While Tortoise lunched upon his liner!

From old Hong Kong, it wasn't long
before our Hare got going again.
He asked around and soon he found
**a clumpy, bumpy
aeroplane...**

For seven days
       he crossed the ocean
flying with a lurching motion,
so it wasn't really any wonder
that he ended
        up

    "Down
        Under."

Now kangaroos are jumpy things,
(I think their feet are made of springs)
so when poor Hare
gave them a scare
by falling on them
from thin air,
they thumped and bumped
him up and down
and quickly bounced him
out of
town.

Undaunted,
Hare soon made his way...

...across the water

until one day...

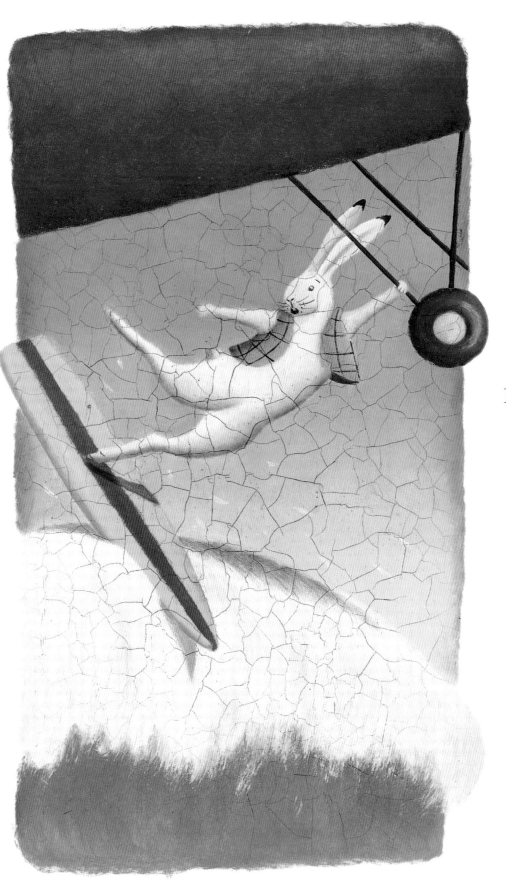

He found himself
aboard again
a roaring, soaring
aeroplane.
(well, almost!)

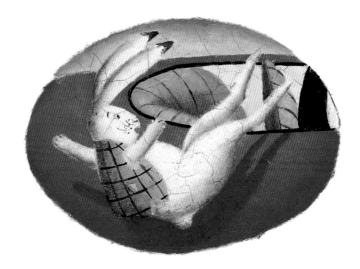

Hare was setting record time.

    He cried,

"This race
is surely mine!"

but sadly our hero didn't see
Tortoise **waiting** at Liberty!

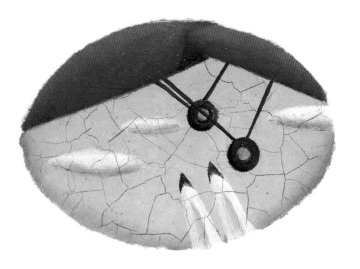

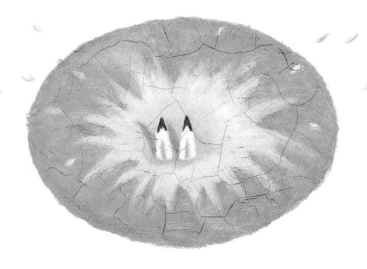

And so at last, fed-up and beaten
Hare was forced to admit defeat,
and what was worse was having to know
he'd lost to someone terribly slow.

And as for the moral, as Aesop would say–
slow and steady
wins the day!

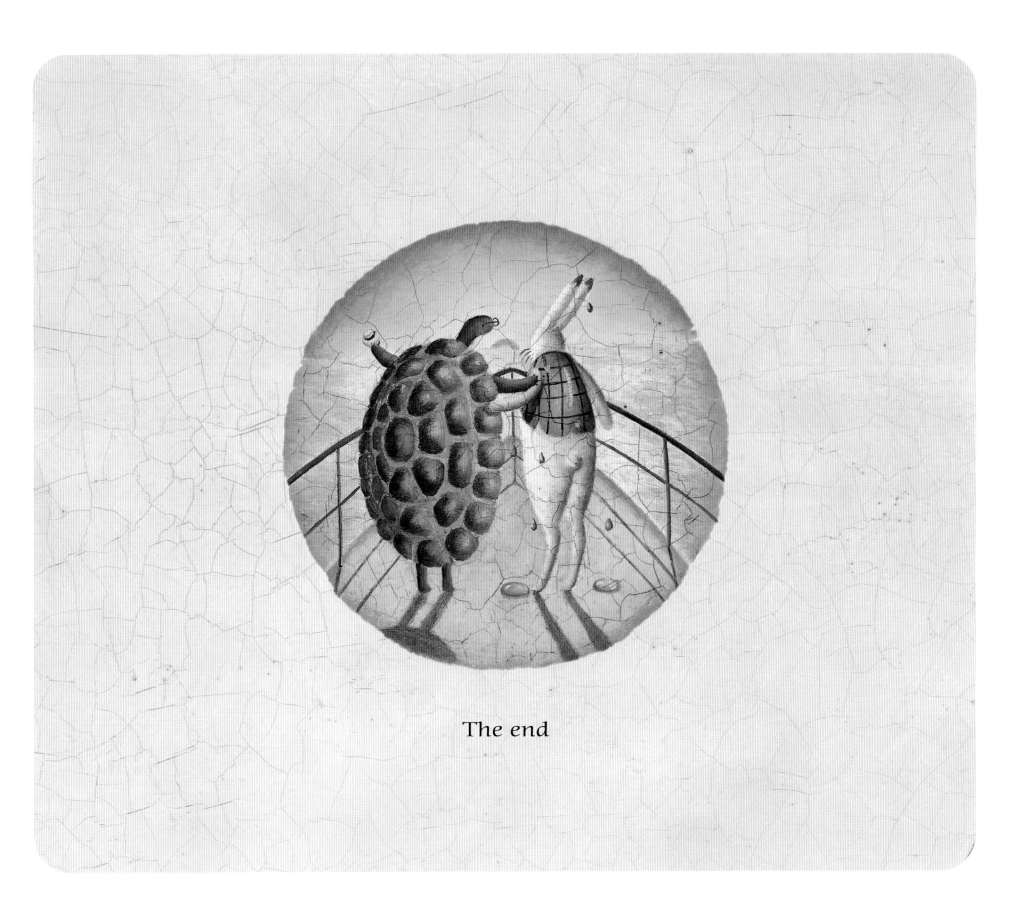

The end